Do You Want to Be Happy Now?

Wendy Ann Zellea

Happy Awareness Publications, LLC

http://AscensionMessages.com
http://AnEnlightenedAuthor.com
wendy@AscensionMessages.com

Do You Want to Be Happy Now?

WENDY ANN ZELLEA

New Era Edition

DEDICATION

This book is dedicated to my Mother, for teaching me to laugh, whenever possible...
My father, for teaching me how to wonder....
And to those enlightened friends and beings I have met on my journey.

PREFACE

*Our thoughts become a tangled ball of yarn,
throughout our life, until we gain awareness. Then,
thread-by-thread, carefully and patiently we begin to
untangle the threads and weave them into a beautiful
scarf, which will keep us warm and comfortable and make
our life better. Be of Good Cheer...*

--Martin William Zellea

CONTENTS

INTRODUCTION

I have always been happy. Perhaps not every moment, but most of my life. I always thought everyone else was happy too, but alas…

What I wish, is that I could do something to help those who are unhappy, get happy. So, I try to make others laugh whenever I can.

This is a simple book, and I intended it to be that way. Hopefully, bits and pieces of it will help those who honor my work by reading it, to find a way to feel happier.

Written with much Love and Light,
Wendy Ann Zellea

BEING HAPPY

The purpose of life is to be happy. That is why we are here. We spend much of our time pursuing what we believe will make us happy, but sometimes we fail to realize that happiness is a feeling, and just thinking about what makes us happy will give us the feeling. We only need the thought and we will experience the happiness.

If we want a new job, we can imagine that we already have it, and are learning the salary we desire. By doing so, we already have the feeling of happiness the new position will offer, even before it happens. In addition, focusing on the desired outcome, will allow it to manifest more easily.

Of course, we still want to get the job, since we cannot go shopping with our feelings. At that point, all we must do is to allow it to materialize and take the steps we feel are necessary to make it happen. That may include brushing up on skills, so that when an interview comes around, we are prepared.

A sense of accomplishment, opportunity to work at something we love, and the increased income associated with our new job, can be created by our thoughts. Thoughts are real and can attract situations into our lives. On the other hand, once we already have the happy feeling, we might decide we like our current job.

Either way we cannot lose, for no matter what the outcome, we are happy.

INTENTION

Man must pass from the competitive to the creative mind; he must form a clear mental picture of the things he wants, and hold this picture in his thoughts with the fixed PURPOSE to get what he wants, and the unwavering FAITH that he does get what he wants, closing his mind against all that may tend to shake his purpose, dim his vision, or quench his faith…

Wallace Wattles

***

First, we must have the intention. Then we can proceed.

FIRST, WE ARE HAPPY

We are all born happy. As very young children, we play, laugh, and giggle throughout the day. We do not need anyone to tell us what we like or do not like, and we are willing to throw a tantrum to get our way.

We eat what we choose and do as we please, resisting anything, without hesitation, that does not suit our fancy. When we become unhappy, we protest wholeheartedly by crying, kicking, screaming, or trying to run away.

Happiness is so essential to us, that we are willing to devote one hundred percent of our energy into anything that helps us maintain our happy state. If we want a toy and it is given to us, we are delighted and completely content. If the plaything is taken away, it becomes an overwhelming tragedy.

As we get older, we often learn to set aside what we truly desire. We learn that there are things we *must* do, whether we like it or not -- that is just the way life is. However, it is not the way life is supposed to be.

We do not have to accept or settle for anything. We only must have the intention to be happy, remember how it feels to be happy, and decide that we will remain happy. Yes, it is *that* simple! So, now we know how to feel happy, but what is true happiness?

OUR HIGHER SELF

Everything in this book is true. At least it was true for me when it was written. Beliefs may be true for some and not for others. It is up to each of us to decide what we believe. We are the only ones who know our own truth. The way we know is through our feelings.

There are different types of feelings. One type is created by emotions, which are fed by the ego. Another is *knowing*, which is fed by our intuition. *Knowing* is what we believe at a soul level. Others may think they know what is right for us, but it is only based on what is true for them. If a person tells us something that we think is right for us, we can use our feelings to determine whether we agree.

Even if we are not certain about what is in our best interest, the Higher Self knows everything. The Higher Self receives information from the Higher Realms, information that is essential for us to live a full and happy life as we continue on our Spiritual Path.

The Higher Self is the luminous being, having a human experience as us, and projecting that experience into the world. The nature of our Higher Self is to be happy; so, when we are communicating with our Higher Self, as we did when we were very young, we are happy. When we do not listen to our inner guidance, we are more likely to experience struggle.

When we quiet our minds and listen to the *whisperings*, we are in tune with the Rhythm of Life and consciously connected to our Higher Self.

In mainstream society, it is hardly mentioned that this higher guidance exists and that we have access to it. When we begin our conscious Spiritual journey, we begin to realize that it is all about reconnecting with our Higher Self. As we do this, we once again become aware of the connection the Higher Self has with the Higher Beings that are waiting to assist us.

A New Era of Conscious Human Evolution has begun. Thanks to the Internet and social media, enlightened ways of thinking are more accessible. Truths that have been forgotten for ages, are popping up like weeds through the cracks. Ancient Codes are embedded in this new information, inspiring us to think differently, as we walk life's path as spiritual seekers. In addition, a growing awareness and remembrance of our connection to primal Sacred Sites is escalating the process of Conscious Human Evolution, by awakening the vibrations of the pristine, ancient wisdom that once kept the world in balance, and is stored in our cellular memory. Welcome to the New Era.

In the natural world, the seasons come and go, life continues perfectly and effortlessly. The sun does not struggle to rise, or the tide exert an effort to roll in or out. There is no conflict when flowers bloom or lions roar. Nature occurs and flows, and as part of nature, so do we.

When we are aligned with our Higher Self, we are certain of our path in life. Even if we are not sure of what it is, we *know* we are on it. There is synchronicity and flow. Answers to questions present themselves, almost magically. We are in touch with our guidance. It feels natural for us to know what to do in all situations. Things work out well, sometimes not always the way we imagined, but we believe that the results of our actions will produce the best outcome.

All living things are pleasure seeking. It is how life continues. When this becomes our norm, and we are attracted only to uplifting feelings and thoughts, we can set our intention to be happy, healthy, and have no problems. If we are not sure of our path in life, we can begin a process of eliminating what no longer serves us. We can start to do things our own way. It may be lonely at times, but the reward is that we are living our life as it is meant to be lived. After a while, it will become easier and we will begin to see that there is no need for struggle. We are all amazing beings, and when we take a chance to follow our own mind, it is a happy feeling.

BEING HAPPY?

What does it mean to be happy? It means we are not unhappy. This answer is not just an exercise in semantics, but rather the elucidation of the very essence of happiness, a state of being which seeks to avoid unhappiness. Since we are all born happy, it can be assumed that somewhere along the way, we learned unhappiness. Therefore, in order to return to a happy state, unhappiness must be un-learned.

No one can make us happy, and no one can make us unhappy. We may think that others are making us unhappy, but that is only because we are reacting to their unhappiness. This is not to minimize life situations that are truly painful, but in the New Era it is essential to remain an observer and realize that each individual is on their own path. We must allow them to be on that path. We may be able to offer assistance, and we can always send Love.

Feeling sorry for others increases their victimization, which adds to their suffering. If we wish to help someone, we can focus on a solution to the problem and imagine they are living a happy, healthy life. On some level they will be, for we are focusing on a reality where the problem does not exist. In doing so, we are sending them positive vibes, which will attract increased higher energy to the overall situation.

The best thing we can do, for ourselves or anyone, is to envision a world where people are happy and well. When we are happy, we see the world from a holistic point of view, consisting of infinite situations and possibilities for everyone. As we maintain that worldview, we are helping to create such a reality.

One excuse for not being happy is that some folks do not believe in happiness. They do not see many happy people and feel that it is only a pipe dream. Over time, they do not even know what happiness means. Even if nobody else is happy, it does not mean we have to follow. Remember, we started off happy and we forgot how to be so. We live in a world where we have the opportunity to be happy. We are supposed to be happy. We are meant to be happy.

We might say, that we will *try* to be happy, but there is no such thing as trying. When we try something, we are giving ourselves permission to fail.

Try not. Do, or do not. There is no try.

Yoda, Star Wars V

When the famous Native American photographer Edward S. Curtis first went to Alaska, he noted: *The children and adults alike of the Nunivak group are…exceptionally happy, because they have been little affected by contact with civilization.*

Being unhappy is learned, and some people are quite good at it. We do not want to become so accustomed to unhappiness that we accept it as our normal state. If we dare to dream that we are happy, we will remain so.

Ok, so now we have gone beyond *trying* to be happy and have decided that we are *going to be* happy. Another mistake! Instead, it is better to decide that we *are* happy, not that we *are going to be* happy. It makes no sense to put it off to the future. What about NOW? Now is when we are creating our future.

Even if we don't believe at first that we are happy, we can just keep thinking that it is true, and over time we will convince our brain that it is. The brain does not know if our thoughts are true or not, it only produces chemicals and creates neural pathways that correspond to our thoughts. Its job is to send the chemicals to receptors on our cells. When we believe we are happy, our cells are receiving happy chemicals so, we will feel happy.

Yes, it is true, our thoughts create our reality. If we think we are nice, then we will be. If we dislike the way we look, our appearance will reflect that. If we think we are beautiful, we are.

We must forget about criticizing ourselves and comparing ourselves to others. We are what we *are*. We are perfect. By making ourselves flawed, we are not liking ourselves just the way we are. When we are happy, we Love ourselves

NOW, with or without the twenty pounds. We are the same person either way.

The only difference is we weigh a different amount. We each have the choice to be happy or unhappy, but whatever choice we make, we are always the same person. The only thing that changes is how well we think of ourselves and how much we know ourselves.

When we are happy, we only have positive thoughts about ourselves. When we look in the mirror, we see how good we look, we do not criticize. Why should we? By what standard are we judging? Besides, we have created what we are. If we want to improve, then we can change.

We are all on the same journey through life. Wherever we are right now, is where we are supposed to be. We must decide which aspects of ourselves we love and let go of the rest. Soon we will only have loving thoughts. It is a happy feeling.

HAVING IT OUR WAY

When we want to say *no*, we can say it, and when we want to say *yes*, we can say that as well. A child does not hesitate to say *yes* or *no*. As children, we were honest with our word. Of course, there are different ways to say something, and the best way is to express ourselves in a kind manner.

How wonderful we felt as children, when we discovered we could say *no*. The world was ours. Everything was going to be our way, exactly how we wished. What could be better?

All our little life, people told us *no*. Now we had joined the *no* club. However, the joy was short-lived.

We listened to others when they said *no*, but the same result was not achieved when we said it back. In fact, quite the opposite happened. When we said no, sometimes our mother or father became angry. We tried a few more times to say no, but after a while, we stopped. That was when we became disconnected from our feelings. We began to believe that since we could not say *no*, why bother. Instead, we decided that it was easier to do what others expected of us, so we could get their approval. After a while, we stopped thinking about what we truly wanted, no less trying to achieve it.

Then came the teenage years, when our desires began to re-surface. The choice before us as teenagers was either to continue to do what our parents, and the world, expect of us, to follow our friends, or to do what we believed was right. Almost all of us go a little wild in our teenage years, the degree to which is determined by our personality and how repressed we were.

It was the time of life when we had the opportunity to become unique beings or to follow the crowd. Those of us who choose to be individuals will be loners and those who follow others will have the approval of our peers and perhaps our family. The rewards of approval are diminished by the separation we have from our selves when we follow the crowd. The loneliness of those of us who choose to go our own way is lessened by the feelings of fulfillment from being connected to ourselves. In order for us to be happy, it is essential to follow our own beliefs. The teenage years are the testing grounds and the years following are the proving grounds.

We must get to the root of what we truly desire and do what makes us happy. Why not? If we never try, we will never know.

THE TRUTH

If an entire planet of people believes something is true, it becomes collectively accepted. However, if one person does not consider it to be true, then is it still absolutely true? At some point in history, people began to believe that men were superior to women, people must grow old, the New Year begins on January 1st, and the list goes on. Many of these beliefs came about at the same time across the planet in groups of people who had no contact with each other. This is because all life forms communicate telepathically.

Those of us who view ourselves as civilized, see others, who have retained their old ways, as backward. We fail to remember that at one time we were the same. In the future, there will be advanced civilizations that look at the current accepted wisdom, as old-fashioned. To future societies, which use technology to create a clean, healthy environment, our current culture will seem unenlightened.

There was a time when people thought the Earth was flat, a concept that is now inconceivable. Quantum Physicists are discovering that a theory such as Dualism, which has been the fundamental basis of modern physics, is not necessarily true, after all. Cutting-edge archeologists are determining that human history is *at least* ten thousand years older than traditionally thought.

We are not separate from everything in the Universe. In fact, we are connected to *all that is*. It does no good to look upon past beliefs as backward, because they were essential stepping-stones to more evolved ways of thinking. Instead, we can be thankful for the progress and the lessons that we have learned. We can also be happy that we are living in the *Now*, experiencing the wonders of life.

We should be grateful for our life, and everything in it. This is important, because gratitude signifies acceptance, and validates the act of receiving. Once we have acknowledged and given thanks for what we have, we are in the position to receive more, so it is helpful to express genuine gratitude whenever possible. We will feel happy when we are grateful, and grateful that we are happy.

We can always look for uplifting aspects in a situation. When we hear doubtful thoughts trying to creep in, telling us that things probably will not work, or it is too good to be true, we can just let them go. They are surfacing from deep within us. Those thoughts are moving from our subconscious into our conscious, so that we may release them. *Better out than in*, I say.

Gratitude is felt in varying degrees. Imagine walking outside for a long time, on a very hot day and being extremely thirsty. There is no water available. As you continue to walk, knowing it will be quite some time before there is someplace to buy water, the thought of a drink of water sounds better and better. Finally, you buy a cold bottle of water and begin to drink. It is so refreshing, you enjoy it more than any other drinking experience you can remember.

Now imagine sitting at home with a glass of water and taking a sip because you are mildly thirsty. You may hardly feel grateful for the sip of water since it was only a slight matter of comfort.

Gratitude is not just a passing feeling that we experience in hopes we will attract more. When we can sincerely express genuine gratitude for what we already have in our life, we will create an environment of abundance.

When we Love every aspect of life right now, each step, even if we trip, is one more step towards our goals, hopes, and dreams. The thoughts and actions of our daily life are the building blocks of our future and we determine the quality our creation.

KNOWING

Modern science is the standard by which new ideas are validated. Unless something has been studied and proven to be true by scientifically trained individuals, it is usually not considered valid or valuable knowledge. However, modern science has only been around for a relatively short time, in the history of the Earth, so why is it the ultimate source of truth?

Intuitive knowledge and natural wisdom are the original, genuine, valid sources of information, yet they are disregarded and looked upon as conjecture, often resulting in a loss of valuable wisdom. Recent discoveries have shown that societies, more advanced than ours, flourished on Earth many thousands of years ago. Therefore, it is safe to assume that the current method of science, is not the only one that is valid.

The ability to create wisdom and truth has been delegated to a group of people, whose job it is to validate our existence. Scientists are not divine. They use a specific process to prove theories that do not need proof for anyone who has faith in life and a connection with *Source*.

However, in all fairness, we must acknowledge scientists for leading the way to the enhancement of modern life through the development and refinement of technology, without which the world would be one of physical struggle, as it still is for many.

Science is only valid within the boundaries of scientific method. Suppose there is one person, who believes that time is not time, and that we can step out of time. Perhaps one day we are late for work and decide not to look at the clock, but rather measure time the way we wish. In other words, we slow down time so that we are not late. We then get to work on time, because we stepped out of the accepted system of time and then back into it. Then is time really time? Try it some time.

It is said that we can look at a cloud and choose to erase it from the sky. If we do, is that cloud still there for someone else? In order to erase the cloud, first we must believe we can do it. If George Lucas can conceive of the powers of the Jedi, is it possible that they truly exist? Do thoughts alone create reality? Considering that there are people who have claimed to erase clouds and alter time, then what is REALLY true? Is truth only what a majority decides to call reality?

Do fictional beings exist in other dimensions, as surely as those who do in the Third Dimension? Perhaps there was a time when humans lived at a different vibration, one of peace and harmony. If it can be envisioned, then it must be possible. What if possibilities are just realities in other dimensions? When we look in a wooded area, do we sense beings? Are those beings looking back at us?

If we take a chance and think outside the box, we can experience reality in a new way. Who knows what else can be achieved, when we are willing to dare to dream. The world could use some REALLY new ideas and beliefs, ideas of the magnitude of the Earth being round instead of flat. Think how happy we would be if we discovered something entirely fantastic and new. Why set our sights any lower?

Technology is continuously developing and evolving. There are software programmers developing applications that are hacked by other developers. Then programmers must create even more advanced software to fight the hackers, and on and on. Each idea is a stepping-stone to the next level.

There is an ancient wisdom that remains true throughout the ages. This is the wisdom that was given to us to live and thrive here on Earth. Let us embrace it once again and return to our path.

Belief systems extend to all areas of life, including the choice of a life partner, the way we treat others, child rearing, concepts of divinity, and the connection we have with ourselves and the universe. If we do not determine what we truly believe, blindly accepting the conventions of the society in which we live, we will be rendered less powerful. Living according to what we *know* to be true will make us happy. It is that simple!

FUN

Everyone loves to have fun. When we have fun, we are happy. There is no specific time for fun, such as Saturday or Sunday afternoon. Any time, which is appropriate, should be devoted to fun.

Fun is so much fun! Fun makes us happy and makes us smile and laugh. When we think of something that is fun, capture the feeling, and remember it, we can always return to it and feel happy. When we take every opportunity to have as much fun as possible, it adds to our happiness.

SELF ESTEEM

Self-esteem is the opinion we have of ourselves. Healthy self-esteem is essential to happiness. Self-esteem can be measured by how well we treat ourselves and those close to us. It determines the outlook we have towards every aspect of life. Loving ourselves, allows us the joy of thinking how wonderful we are.

In the modern world, self-esteem can become diminished as we are constantly bombarded with unattainable ideals, intended to turn us into perpetual consumers of products that are supposed to help us reach those ideals. All too often it works. We buy into it, literally. A better choice is to set our own standards and feel good about ourselves for doing so.

When we listen to the mainstream, self-diminishing, information stream, it leads us to measure our self-worth by what we own and how we look. We become characterized by a car, clothes, a house, and a myriad of toys. This can result in buying products, which we hope will compensate for a lack of personal fulfillment. There is nothing wrong with owning things, but *stuff* will not make us happy. We must be happy first and then get all the *stuff* we want. We will find, at that point, we may not want as much *stuff* as we originally thought.

When we begin to examine all our excellent qualities, and then keep our focus on those qualities, we can develop more desirable character traits. The unnecessary ones will fade away when we do not give them our attention.

We do not require anyone else's approval, only our own. We are a reflection of the Divine energy of the Universe, and we can rise to it.

All of us are capable of making good decisions for ourselves. We do not have to do what everyone else does, and then blame society when things do not turn out the way we expected. Even if our choices are unique, we can trust that they are appropriate for us. We do not have to follow the crowd, do things, or go places, just because we think we should, when it is not what we really want to do. Instead, we can allow ourselves to do what we *feel like doing*, instead of what we think we *should* do.

The same way we would feel if someone told us that they did not trust us, is the way we will feel, in our center or Solar Plexus, if we do not have confidence in ourselves. When we believe in ourselves, and the wonderful journey of life, we attract people who also believe in us. As we begin to trust ourselves, we are happy.

THERE'S NO COMPARISON

Comparing ourselves to others implies a lack of trust in ourselves. What another person *is*, *does*, or *has*, should not matter to us at all. Very often the person to whom we are comparing ourselves is not as we think they are. When we observe that they have more money than us, a nicer car, are better looking, or have a better body, we are focusing on something, which we believe is lacking in ourselves. This will only attract more lack.

Whatever qualities we have, without them, we could never hope to learn the lessons we are meant to learn. We might as well accept ourselves the way we are, since that is the way we are, whether we accept it or not.

When we criticize another person, we are really criticizing ourselves. We find a fault in someone, because we believe we have a corresponding one. That is what makes us notice the shortcoming in them. Instead of finding fault with another person, we can look inward to see if personal growth is possible.

On the other hand, if we believe we are more attractive, richer, or smarter than someone else, we are using them to validate those things for which we feel ourselves superior. This translates into insecurity and lack of self-esteem and will only attract more of the same.

When we are happy, we do not see any faults in ourselves or anyone else, instead we see the perfection of everyone. We do not think of comparing ourselves to someone else. Doing so is only an attempt to make us feel superior to them. We are hoping to outdo the person to whom we are making the comparison. We want to be smarter, better-looking, richer, or in some way cooler than they are. It is an exercise in futility, since we are the judge of which of us is the better part of the comparison.

When we are happy, we know there is no point in comparing, because everyone is exactly how he or she should be. No one is better than anyone else. We are only at different places on our journey through life. Yes, we are perfectly where we are supposed to be, so instead, we can Love where we are and BE HAPPY!

HAPPINESS AND WELL-BEING

Healing is the process of restoring the physical, emotional, and spiritual condition to its default state. It is returning to the natural state of well-being. It is bringing back balance to the life form. Our bodies are the expression of our feelings, just as the environment is the expression of the state of being of its inhabitants.

Humans have moved into the New Era. When we embrace the inevitable changes that lie ahead, we are able to fearlessly proceed, with a sense of wonder, into the unknown. It is then that we will experience paradise.

We all require nurturing, whether from ourselves or from others. When we are not sufficiently nurtured, we may create situations that demand it. Nurturing sustains the conditions, which encourage, support, and promote both physical and spiritual wellness. In the New Era, the importance of self-nurturing is accepted as a means of sustaining well-being.

An excellent way we can nurture ourselves is by doing nothing, in other words relaxing. Doing nothing is really doing something. Taking bubble baths, meditating, doing yoga, travelling, living life in the moment, all help us to be happy.

Clearing our physical and mental space is essential for happiness. Everything we have stuffed away in a closet is catalogued in our brain and taking up space. Getting rid of clutter, meaning getting rid of what we no longer use, things we no longer like, items we would not buy now, and all that does not resonate with the energy of the New Era.

When we allow outdated aspects of ourselves to dissolve and fade away, the result is an increased sense of happiness and accelerated Spiritual Growth. When the clutter is gone, and we replace the old stuff with happy thought forms such as peace, love, tranquility, kindness, and joy, energy will flow, and we will glow.

DON'T WORRY, BE HAPPY

When we stop *worrying*, our happiness will increase. Worrying is a complete waste of time. If we worry about something and it works out, we worried for nothing. If we worry about something and it does not work out, we only made the situation worse by placing our focus on a result we do not want, thereby helping to create it.

Worrying wastes huge amounts of energy. When we allow events to unfold, envisioning the best outcome, we are using our energy to create the results we desire. If we are happy, we have faith that things will turn out well and that the universe will provide solutions. As things continually work out for the best, we will see the magic of life.

How do we stop worrying? First, we must have that intention, and then realize we are in control of our thoughts. We do not have to worry about anything. Worrying is a habit we learned. We did not worry as children. Why should anything go wrong? Life is not supposed to be full of things going wrong.

IT'S ALWAYS SOMETHING

It's always something is a popular phrase, but it's not always something. That concept is counter-productive. If we believe *it's always something*, it will be. If we believe that things go smoothly, then they will.

Consider nature, everything is perfect in the natural world and everyone is part of that world. Why then should we experience mishap after mishap? When we say that it is always something, we are not allowing ourselves to believe that things can go well. We are in opposition to the natural flow of life. When we go with the flow, we see life unfold perfectly, the way it is meant to. When we hear someone say, *it's always something*, we know *it is not.*

NO REGRETS

Regret is another waste of time and energy, the same as worrying. We cannot change something that happened or what we or someone else did. So why throw away our energy regretting it? When we regret something, we are still putting energy and thoughts into what we are regretting. We are still participating in and sustaining events we wish had occurred differently or had never happened.

Over time, if we continue to regret things, we will end up regretting the time we spent regretting. When we are happy, we will not regret anything because we know that everything happened to get us to our happy state.

When we say or think the phrase *with my luck*, we are not trusting in life. Instead, we are increasing the chance of attracting whatever it is we do not desire. There is no such thing as luck anyway, because we are the ones creating our own reality.

STRESSED OUT

Oh, stress, that which makes us feel so important, sophisticated, and successful. Oh, to be stressed out, with a cell phone to our ear, seeming so busy and essential. Stress is not our friend, nor is it a mark of success. It cannot make us feel important or valuable. What it does is make us unwell and unhappy.

What is stress? There is more than one definition, depending on the context in which the word is used. Physics defines stress as *the internal distribution of forces within a body that balance and react to the loads applied to it.* In other words, the point to which something can be pushed. Emotionally, stress is the point beyond which we can comfortably be pushed. It is the opposite of relaxation. It is there to tell us that we are going too far, pushing too hard, and wasting energy unnecessarily.

It is not natural to be overly stressed. Does the sun stress to rise in the morning or the moon to travel through its phases each month? Do the creatures of the Earth stress in our natural environment? Of course, they do not. Stress is so popular now it has become a normal part of daily life.

Stress is the primary cause of illness. When we hold stress in our physical or emotional spheres, we create blocks, which prevent life force energy from flowing freely. When this happens, the body cannot function or heal itself properly, since well-being can only be achieved in a relaxed state.

So, we must lighten up, unwind, and let the energy flow so that we can be happy. Techniques such as Reiki, meditation, Yoga, massage, walking, along with a long list of other relaxing activities, all promote wellness by reducing the stress in our body, mind, and spirit. These activities allow the natural healing, balancing, and restorative capabilities of our energy body to function as designed.

If we dwell on the daily, mainstream news that is filled with unfortunate happenings, it lowers our energy level and creates stress. If we must listen, we can do it objectively. There are many encouraging things happening every day, fantastic advances in the emotional and spiritual evolution of humanity. Books, movies, music, and being in nature, all can make us happy and lift our spirits. When we tune into the positive aspects of daily life, we are advancing ourselves.

SHOULD WE?

What should we do? There is that pesky *should* word. Every time we hear or speak it, whatever follows is not our true desire. There are infinite *shoulds*. *Should* implies that we do not want to do what we are saying we *should* do. When we say it, we are ignoring our Higher Self and doing what we believe others would want us to do. In other words, we are giving up our power, operating from guilt, and not listening to our feelings. A better idea is to do what resonates with us.

When we pursue our true passion, life is exciting. We do not become stressed when we are doing what we Love. Being focused on what we Love and devoting time to our interests, keeps our minds active and happy.

FOOD

Eating is fun, or at least it should be, considering all the choices of food we have available to us. Overeating is not fun and is the cause of excess weight. The cause of overeating is emotional.

When we eat healthy food, which we feel like eating, we feel good. We do not have to deprive ourselves, just eat less of certain things. The time to eat is when we are hungry. The time to stop, is when we are not hungry anymore. The body wants food, not chemicals. It's all very simple.

We do not have to count every calorie and gram of fat we put in our mouth. By dissecting every mouthful into nutritional categories, we are turning eating into a homework assignment. Instead, we can eat *real* food to nourish the body.

Thinness is the current cultural preference and an obsession for many. It is not an ideal based on absolute truth. Painting and sculptures from other periods in history, which portray the subjects as well-rounded and robust, are proof of that. When we are in tune with our body and eat only what it requires, we will achieve the ideal size. Keep in mind, that ideal size may not necessarily be skinny.

To get the most from our food, we must Love what we eat. The thoughts and energy we send towards what we consume determines the benefit we will receive from those substances.

If we choose to eat out of guilt, wishing we could be eating something else, the food will not be synthesized into the nourishment we require. On the other hand, if we Love what we eat, know it is nutritious and that it will add to our well-being, the energy of that food will resonate with our body.

When we Love what we eat, we will be happy and thankful for our food. Breathing, eating, drinking water, and sleeping are sacred activities. When we eat and drink with gratitude, love, grace, and respect, we experience increased benefits from all that we consume. As we eat only the best food and drink the purest water, the body will respond by giving us a healthy life in return.

GETTING REAL

We are part of nature. We are not meant to be constantly in artificial environments such as our home, car, workplace, or the mall. By doing so, we become somewhat disconnected from life.

Granted, many times we have no choice. Our lifestyle or the weather can keep us inside, but we can take the time to glance at the clouds or stop to watch the sunset or the moonrise. We can notice the birds on the telephone wires and listen to them speaking to us.

We are all part of the most glorious aspect of life, the natural world. Looking into the woods on the side of the road when we stop at a red light or taking the time to stop for five minutes at a park on a beautiful day to breathe in the smell of the trees, can bring us closer to nature. Feeling the spirit of the natural world even for a moment is revitalizing. As we connect to nature, we receive information, which helps to re-program and restore us to an enhanced state of well-being.

The environment is our home. Allowing it to be abused is a statement that reflects a collective attitude towards life, the world, and reality. It would be unthinkable to care for our home the way we have treated the Earth, but our disconnection from the *source of life* has allowed this to happen.

Indigenous people would not think of such a thing. They live in harmony with nature and realize it is their means of survival. Nowadays, many of us are separated from the natural world. We are not in harmony with the cycles of the moon, do not look at the clouds during the day, or the moon and stars at night.

Recycling and the slow development of alternative fuel sources are steps in the right direction, but as with any problem, it is essential to get to the source if the Earth is to be restored to its pristine state. It has been claimed numerous times by many people that we create our own reality. Such is the case with the condition of the environment. It cannot be expected that the Earth will be happy when humanity is not.

When we are happy, we see the splendor of the natural world. We look at nature every chance we get. We appreciate and connect with the clouds, the moon, trees, birds, and all of the Earth's beauty. We do not see a garbage dump, we see the flowers growing from it. We never tire of the glory of a sunset or moonrise. We feel as though we are part of the natural world. We are aware of issues but focus on solutions. We send loving energy to the Earth, helping it to heal. Imagine if everyone respected the planet and lived in a way that only sustained the natural balance. When we Love the Earth, and take actions that will sustain it, we are solving environmental issues. When we love anything, it begins to heal.

If we are thinking, *oh, if it were only that simple*, know that it is, but it takes the participation of everyone. If we are thinking, that will never happen, how do we know? If we can do it, so can others. It begins with us, when we allow ourselves to believe it will happen.

AS YEARS GO BY

Being old is a state of mind. It can occur at any age. Each phase of life is as wonderful as the rest, but it is up to us to make it so. When we are happy, age is only a number, not a rule for measuring our value.

We live in a culture that worships youth, disdaining those they see as old. Not long ago in our society, and all along in many other cultures, elders were respected, revered, and held in high esteem and awe.

How long are we really meant to live? There are tales of those who lived hundreds of years. Currently, there are places on Earth where people live well over a hundred years and are still vibrant. Science attributes this to the climate and the diet, but perhaps it is due to their beliefs about aging? It might be better not to think about aging at all and just live life day by day.

When wrinkles appear, we can Love them, because they are part of us. It is only society that labels signs of aging as something to dislike, and what do they know? When we are happy, we embrace aging. Actually, we do not often think about it. We are just happy!

ALL OF US

When we listen to others, we are honoring
them, even if we don't agree. Bowing out of the
conversation, when we don't want to listen
anymore, is honoring ourselves. Because we
don't have to win. And we don't have to be right.
The fact is, we *are* right. We're right for us. Even
if we are wrong, it gives us the opportunity to
change. When we are happy, we do not feel that
we must convince anyone to agree with us.

We are made up of many parts. There is no quantified value to be placed on these parts, we are just pieces of a whole being. Ideally, we are in balance. We do not want to be too lazy, and we do not want to work too hard either.

In order to nurture any relationship, we must look for the aspects of the other person that we admire. As we get to know them, we begin to see their different parts. If we like enough of what we see in the other person, we become closer to them.

Some of us are searching for our soul mate, the person with whom our energy most resonates. There are many soul mates for each person, but normally a relationship is formed with the first one we meet. Coupling and remaining together is our customary, accepted social system. It is a lovely system, which produces beautiful emotional experiences and encourages a high degree of intimacy. It can be a true treasure. When we are in a relationship, we should cherish the opportunity that we have created, for it allows us to participate in a wonderful part of life.

Often, relationships are placed into categories instead of being based upon the connections that truly exist. A relationship is a living thing with its own form. It cannot be forced. It has to be nurtured or it will fade away. *We're either together with someone or we're not.* Some relationships have expiration dates. People come in and out of our lives in cycles.

JUST US

...After all that is bewitching in the idea of a single and constant attachment, and all that can be said of one's happiness depending entirely on any particular person, it is not meant--it is not fit--it is not possible that it should be so...

Jane Austen, Sense and Sensibility

Guess what, we do not have to be in a relationship to be happy. We can be happy just being by ourselves. We do not have to depend on someone to make us happy. What we are able to do is be happy first, and share our happiness with someone, when our paths cross.

IT'S DIVINE

Once we define, we lose the divine.

It is not possible to intellectually define anything that transcends rational thought, especially a divine force. On a grand scale, the divine aspect of life, which is the most important part of our existence, has been partially taken from us and kept hidden beyond reach, somewhere in the sky.

We all come into this world as a part of the Divine universe. Why then do we allow the Divine aspect of ourselves to be given to an outside force? After that, we ask the same *Heavenly Being* to return the Divinity that belonged to us in the beginning.

Would it not be better to have a growing personal relationship with ourselves and become more aware of our limitless, sacred possibilities.

Religions are based on set premises, which participants are expected to believe and follow. Spirituality is a personal belief system, one that allows us to decide what we truly believe. Organized religion separates people in to groups. Spirituality unites everyone as a whole entity.

The belief systems we choose, will either serve us or teach us, so it is essential to determine what we truly believe. Do our beliefs come from within, or do we believe in something more external? When we believe in what fills us with joy, we are uplifted and inspired.

OUR FAMILY

Children are young human beings that are born with the same intelligence as every other person. They are not possessions to be created to keep a relationship together or to prove how much we love someone. They are little beings who deserve as much respect as anyone.

In addition, it is not necessary for us to produce a child to have a happy or meaningful relationship with someone or to prove to ourselves that we are worthy of being alive.

Creating a child should be a thoughtful decision. Not all of us are meant to have a child. On the other hand, if we truly have the desire to be a parent, then a child will bring us much joy and will be a treasure to us.

In today's world, many relationships are no longer meant to last a lifetime. This implies in a new definition of the family unit. Modern families are defined by those we care for as well our relations. A family can also consist of only one person. If we live alone, then we are our family unit.

The most important ingredient in the happiness or success of a family is not the housing arrangements, but the Love that exists amongst the members. Often times a parent shares more quality time with a child when that parent is not living with them.

Families are considered broken or dysfunctional when they do not fit into the traditional family structure, but that is not always the case. A marriage or a relationship that ends has not failed. It has just run its course.

OUR SOUL FAMILY

Soul Families are in a different category altogether. Those of us who are Soul Family members, *know* who our Soul Brothers and Sisters are. It is the recognition of a relationship that is ancient. Members of our Soul Family might be our relatives or may be strangers that we pass on the street. When we meet them, there is no doubt that they remember us, as we remember them.

HAPPY THINGS

Do unto others, as you would have them do unto you.

As children, we learn the Golden Rule, but sometimes we forget to remember it. Consideration for others is fundamental among civilized beings. We will feel good if we treat everyone well, including ourselves.

When someone acts in a way we do not like, that person is only expressing something that is causing them unhappiness. It rarely has anything to do with us. If we respond in the same manner in return, we are allowing them to determine our behavior. We are giving away our power.

We cannot control what others do or say, but we *can* control how we react. Life is not a contest, because we have already won, and the other person has too. That is where our power lies. Therefore, it does not matter if we scream louder or have a cleverer reply. Instead, we can just be happy, whistle a happy tune, and continue on with our day.

Greeting others is a basic, considerate, social interaction. Often a smile or even a nod will do. It is not always possible to greet everyone, but when the opportunity to acknowledge another presents itself, we can take advantage of it. We will see a change in the demeanor of most people when we choose to smile at them. Think of the power we possess, to be able to change the mood of a stranger in a split second just by smiling.

Once we create the habit of smiling at others, we will do it naturally. As we go through our day smiling, we will be projecting and accumulating positive energy, so that by the end of the day we will feel very happy about all the good feelings we have created.

When we walk past someone, we can connect with them for that moment. We have no idea on how many levels we might be relating to that person. Maybe we knew them in another life or a parallel reality. Think of how we would react, if we had not seen anyone in days or weeks. We would be very happy to see another person. Each time we have the opportunity to connect with someone, it is a gift. Smile and be happy.

When we are happy, we take the opportunity to laugh whenever we can. It is truly the best medicine. When we laugh, we release tension and stress, which promotes healing. What could be better? It is fun to make people laugh and everyone feels better afterwards.

Just because we are no longer children, does not mean that we cannot play and enjoy everything we do. Each moment is only there for a moment, then it is gone, and with it goes our chance to be happy in that moment. We have the choice to go through our day either miserable or happy. Either way we will go through the day, so we might as well choose to be happy.

RECEIVING

When we receive, not only are we getting something, which is fun, but we are also allowing someone to give, which makes everyone feel good.

If a person offers us a compliment, we can say thanks, and not diminish it by qualifying it.

When we are happy, we enjoy receiving, for it makes us even happier. Receiving validates the belief that we deserve what has come our way.

Giving and receiving are empowering. As we graciously accept what life brings to us, we will be positioned to receive more.

PASSION

Passion is one of life's treasures. When we are passionate about something, we will be happy doing it. If we are passionately engaged in an activity, we are communicating directly with our Higher Self.

When we look for the things for which we are passionate, and embrace them, we will be happy.

SYNCHRONICITY

Synchronistic events are happening all the time. It is only the awareness of them that increases.

Synchronistic events happen when we are resonating with the diverse vibrations of life. If we were living up to our fullest potential, we would manifest our thoughts instantly. Then we would have to be even more careful what we were thinking.

Synchronistic events are pleasing and magical to those who witness them. Sometimes we may have the experience of thinking of someone just as they call on the phone. Perhaps we even meet by chance on the street. Synchronicity is a comma or pause in life, occurring when multiple events unfold simultaneously. The timing of something is the same as the timing of something else. This is what some call coincidence, but others know it is a gift from the universe. When we embrace these messages, we tend to smile as they happen. We enjoy the fun of receiving a nudge from beyond ordinary reality.

Elevens are another type of synchronistic wink from the universe, as are 22s, 33s, 11:11, and on and on. Nowadays, with digital clocks everywhere, there is more opportunity to see such numbers. It is fun to notice these magical displays of the synchronistic order of the Universe.

IT'S REALLY REAL

We all have our own reality. When enough people agree something is true, it becomes reality for the general population. However, unless everyone believes exactly the same way, there is no such thing as absolute reality.

It is said that some of us are not in touch with reality, but actually, we are all in touch with *some* reality. If our reality is too different from what most people call reality, then we are labelled crazy or eccentric.

The reality of different groups of people, countries, or societies may vary, yet each member of each group, believes that their reality is true and correct, and the reality of the other group not relevant to them.

When we are happy, we are aware that our reality is like a cloud, constantly changing. It is our reality and we will adjust it as we see fit. The changes can be so subtle we may not even notice. When we are happy, we embrace those changes and go with the flow.

ENLIGHTENMENT

We all do the best we can, with what we have to work with at the time. If we think someone can do better, it is only because we are able to see possibilities they cannot. If we were in their shoes, we would be doing the same thing as they are now.

We do not wake up in the morning and say, *I think I will make a conscious effort to make a mess of my life today.* Even though we might know there are better choices for us, we must *have what it takes* to make those choices, not just know of them.

We might have the intellect and skills to do more in life, but not have the confidence that we can accomplish what someone else believes we can. If they tell us what we should be doing or that we are not living up to our potential, they might inspire us to do better, if we are the type of person that listens to advice. In some cases, we might feel threatened and do the opposite of what is suggested. We interpret their suggestions as disapproval instead of encouragement.

What we can do, is be an example in our own life. That way we are not depriving another person of their lessons. It is up to each one of us to either learn what life has in store for us, or not.

Alas, there is no pill we can take to become instantly enlightened. The first, essential step is to be happy. Currently, there is a process of Conscious Human Evolution happening on Earth. Information that has lie dormant for ages, is being broadcast in energetic waves, to those of us who are awakening and ready to receive it.

The excitement that exists over the experience of Higher Consciousness feeds the flow of even more new ideas.

Simply put, there are many people who know that something very new and exciting is happening to the Human Race. There is enthusiasm and anticipation for the next phase of human development. The New Era is creating a subtle, simultaneous dimension that is leading us to a more evolved existence on this planet.

We, as Masters that walk the Earth, have an insatiable appetite for new ideas and information. It is the intensity of emotion involved in the pursuit of new ways of thinking that allows the process to occur undeniably and rapidly. When we realize how lucky we are to live in the New Era, we cannot help but be happy.

HAPPILY BALANCED

The meek shall inherit the Earth.

Many words lose their original meaning and take on new connotations, in various cultures and at different times. The word *meek* has come to imply a person lacking in courage, but it did not always have the same meaning.

Originally, it described a person that was gentle, which by no means has anything to do with cowardice. A gentle soul is a balanced being. In fact, in some cultures, gentleness is sought after, and most admired. In the New Era, gentleness is the default state of a balanced person. It is the *new normal,* thereby demonstrating that the meek, the gentle ones, do inherit the Earth, for it is they that are happily thriving in the new energy.

True power does not come from force. Instead, it generates from focused balance. We experience this when we do Yoga. We must be focused and balanced, so that we can maintain a Yoga posture for a period of time. This type of balance can only occur when we are completely present and grounded. We become aware of the *beyond*, yet we anchor in the n*ow*. We exist in the ebb and flow of a gentle wave of energy washing over us, yet we stay in our center. The same power that creates life itself, fills us. A peaceful feeling envelops us, and we are able resonate, to a greater degree, with Life Force Energy.

It is then that we once again become the Balanced and Gentle Souls we once were, when we incarnated into this lifetime. We no longer feel the need to compete or criticize. We do not require anyone's approval or recognition. In fact, we are traveling on a *Ray of Ascension.*

To some, it may be a sign of weakness, when we are not pushing ahead or taking part in the ego-based, unbalanced, stress-producing activities of the Collective Consciousness. Instead, what we are doing, is listening for guidance, looking for signs, experiencing synchronistic events, and relishing in the flow of life.

This is not just a simplistic description of a person that *is not tuned into* reality. Instead, it is a description of one that *is happy and completely* tuned into reality. Many people are beginning to realize that this vibrational state of mind is attainable, but those of us living in the New Era, have already achieved it.

POSITIVELY HAPPY

Spiritual Growth, otherwise known as becoming enlightened, is a constant process of increasing our energetic signature. Many variables can affect our vibration, such as emotional and environmental factors or even other people. However, there are ways that we can maintain our highest vibration.

Think Positive Thoughts, Speak Positive Words

This may sound like very basic information, but it is so important that it cannot be over emphasized. Each thought and word has a vibration. In fact, everything has a vibration and is made up of energy, which moves in, out, and through our multi-dimensional body, at a rate determined by the level at which we vibrate.

We can resonate with some vibrations and not with others. Our vibration is attracted to, neutral, or repelled by all other vibrations. This is why we are drawn to certain people, colors, music, religion, jobs, and all other aspects of life.

Vibrations are constantly changing, usually so slowly that we normally do not notice. Over time, we may observe that a person has changed somehow, and we no longer feel the same way when we are around them. We may feel uneasy or uncomfortable in their presence. The familiarity that once existed with this person, no longer remains, we either become more distant from them or make changes to the relationship.

The other person may leave for a time, or even forever. On the other hand, we may feel a new sensation and a more loving connection in their company and become even closer. There are many ways one type of energy can interact with another, but it is in our nature to seek out the vibration with which we resonate. In other words, like attracts like.

When thoughts and words are positive, they are life-sustaining, creating an environment for Spiritual Growth. The opposite is also true, negative vibrations do not contribute to our energetic well-being, in fact, they hamper it. So, speaking and thinking positively are the first and most basic steps in our Spiritual Journey.

We can create this energetic environment when we are relaxed or meditative. It is then that we will be happy. When we practice speaking and thinking in positive ways, we begin to see life change for the better.

EVERYTHING OR NOTHING

There is a thinking stuff from which all things are made, and which, in its original state, permeates, penetrates, and fills the interspaces of the universe. A thought, in this substance, produces the thing that is imaged by the thought. Man can form things in his thought, and, by impressing his thought upon formless substance, can cause the thing he thinks about to be created.

In order to do this, man must pass from the competitive to the creative mind; he must form a clear mental picture of the things he wants, and hold this picture in his thoughts with the fixed PURPOSE to get what he wants, and the unwavering FAITH that he does get what he wants, closing his mind against all that may tend to shake his purpose, dim his vision, or quench his faith.

Wallace Wattles

Everything that exists is formed and defined by a thinking substance, which fills the interspaces of the universe. It is called Consciousness. So, what exactly is Consciousness? Consciousness is driven by thoughts, to become reality. It is the stuff from which our thoughts are created and take form. It is *all that is **not**, all which does not exist,* and *all that defines what does exist.* Consciousness is infinite. It is the awareness of it that increases and allows the process of Conscious Evolutionary Growth to occur.

All by which we are defined, is all that we are not.

Even when matter is broken down to its smallest component, there is still something surrounding it, giving it form and shape. When particles of matter are combined in different ways, by the intelligent consciousness that surrounds them, objects are created. This is why there are tables, people, trees, cars, animals, and everything else, which we define as existing. All that does not exist, we call *nothing*. Defining and acknowledging *nothing*, is validating its existence. The undefined space that is labeled *meaningless nothingness*, surrounding and permeating through particles of matter, is what gives form and life to everything. It is The Force that the Jedi revere in Star Wars, and rightly so.

What makes us what we are? We are a collection of particles, atoms, and molecules that are held together by...? We are held together by *nothing*, and *nothing* works perfectly. All the space that surrounds every unit of the matter that forms each individual is what holds us together. The intelligent *nothingness* that gives us life, is all around us and flows through us. Yoda was right.

It has been shown in Quantum physics experiments that when electrons absorb energy, they can jump from one orbit to another. This may seem uneventful at first mention, but there is more to the story. When the electrons make the jump, they start in one orbit and then appear in another. Where do they go in between? They go nowhere and that is where they energize. *Nowhere* is where there is *nothing* and that is where the source of Light and life resides.

Having said all this, it can be seen how silly it is to call the source of Life Force Energy *nothing* and have it reside nowhere. Rational thinkers are determined to view existence in absolute terms. In doing so, they have separated us from the Source of everything. Originally, people were aware of the forces of life that could influence and affect transformation. Ooops, did I just define magic? The "M" word is like a weed. It cannot be stamped out. It always grows up between the cracks and blossoms.

Magic is part of life. When we can smile at someone and transform his or her face into a smile, it is magic. Transformation is part of life. *Nothing*, as it is called, is the source of all magic. As we become aware that we have the power to change our lives by changing the way we think, we find ourselves in situations where we are able to choose our own belief systems, realize our own power, discover we can heal our body, mind, and spirit, and decide to be happy.

When we are happy, we are energized, vitalized, and we know that *nothing* is just as real as something. When we feel a balance between the seen and the unseen, the real and the unreal, something and nothing, we create a state of wellness, for it is then that the Life Force Energy, which sustains us, can flow through us freely. Being happy is the way to create this balance. It is that simple. When we go for it, we will be smiling and happy ... NOW!!!

HOLDING THE LIGHT

There currently exists, and the number is growing, many individuals and groups who realize that their purpose on earth is to contribute to the transformation, transmutation, and evolution of the Earth and its inhabitants…

We are the ones holding the Light for all humanity, and paving the way for all of us to move into the Higher Realms…

It is what we have chosen to do…

It is our destiny…

And it is what matters to us…

And now, more than ever, it is up to each of us to hold as much Light as we can. And Shine it even brighter, so that all the world will not forget that there still is a Light…

The Sacred Masculine and Sacred Feminine energies will be balanced…

And we will again become the Luminous, Enlightened Light Beings we once were…

A MANTRA

We do what we love.

And are grateful for everything in our life.

We follow our feelings,

Speak kind words,

And think happy thoughts.

We are kind. That is all.

We speak positive words.

We think positive thoughts.

No exceptions.

Anything else is not life sustaining.

And So It Is...

ABOUT THE AUTHOR...

Wendy Ann Zellea is an Ascension Messenger, Luminary, and IT Professional. After receiving a degree in English, she left it all behind to become a musician.

In 1984, after a personal tragedy, she moved to Belize, Central America, where she lived for 15 years on a tropical island off the mainland. There she owned and operated a breakfast restaurant.

A few years later she returned to New Jersey, her home, where she began working in Software Development.

Since then, Wendy has published five non-fiction books and a novel. She has written numerous articles, which appear on her websites.

Wendy is a featured speaker at metaphysical events.

Wendy's Websites:

http://AscensionMessages.com

http://AnEnlightenedAuthor.com

BOOKS BY WENDY ANN ZELLEA

* **My Way Around –** *Journeying the Infinite Spiral of Life*
* **Being a Master in the New Era –**
  Integrating the Codes of Ascension
* **Saving Atlantis –** *A Mystical, Modern Myth*
* **Ascension Messages from the Higher Realms –**
  The Process of Human Evolution
* **Life is Good, All is Well – Everything is Vibration -** *New Era Edition*
* **Do You Want to Be Happy NOW? –** *New Era Edition*

Made in the USA
Middletown, DE
29 October 2020

22970064R00085